jazz-rock

Arranged by Brent Edstrom

T0039559

contents

ISBN 978-1-5400-1543-3

HAL•LEONARD®

Visit Hal Leonard Online at
www.halleonard.com

Contact Us:
Hal Leonard
7777 West Bluemound Road
Milwaukee, WI 53213
Email: info@halleonard.com

In Europe contact:
Hal Leonard Europe Limited
Distribution Centre, Newmarket Road
Bury St Edmunds, Suffolk, IP33 3YB
Email: info@halleonardeurope.com

In Australia contact:
Hal Leonard Australia Pty. Ltd.
4 Lentara Court
Cheltenham, Victoria, 3192 Australia
Email: info@halleonard.com.au

AFRICA

Words and Music by DAVID PAICH
and JEFF PORCARO

BABE

Words and Music by
DENNIS DeYOUNG

Moderately slow Jazz Ballad

THE BEST OF TIMES

Words and Music by
DENNIS DeYOUNG

BLACK WATER

Words and Music by
PATRICK SIMMONS

COME SAIL AWAY

Words and Music by
DENNIS DeYOUNG

DEACON BLUES

Words and Music by WALTER BECKER
and DONALD FAGEN

Moderately fast Swing

DO IT AGAIN

Words and Music by WALTER BECKER
and DONALD FAGEN

A HORSE WITH NO NAME

Words and Music by
DEWEY BUNNELL

Moderately slow Swing

31

LISTEN TO THE MUSIC

Words and Music by
TOM JOHNSTON

Medium New Orleans Swing groove

THE LOGICAL SONG

Words and Music by RICK DAVIES
and ROGER HODGSON

MARRAKESH EXPRESS

Words and Music by
GRAHAM NASH

Light and rhythmic Swing

MORE THAN A FEELING

Words and Music by
TOM SCHOLZ

PICK UP THE PIECES

Words and Music by JAMES HAMISH STUART,
ALAN GORRIE, ROGER BALL,
ROBBIE McINTOSH, OWEN McINTYRE
and MALCOLM DUNCAN

REELING IN THE YEARS

Words and Music by WALTER BECKER
and DONALD FAGEN

ROSANNA

Words and Music by
DAVID PAICH

RIKKI DON'T LOSE THAT NUMBER

Words and Music by WALTER BECKER
and DONALD FAGEN

ROCK WITH YOU

Words and Music by
ROD TEMPERTON

SPINNING WHEEL

Words and Music by
DAVID CLAYTON THOMAS

SUITE: JUDY BLUE EYES

Words and Music by
STEPHEN STILLS

TAKE THE LONG WAY HOME

Words and Music by RICK DAVIES
and ROGER HODGSON

Moderately fast Swing

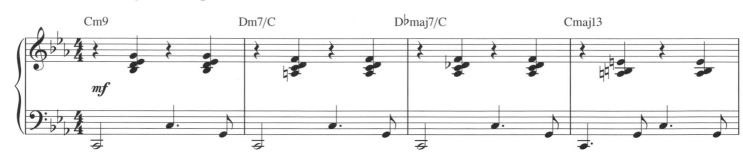

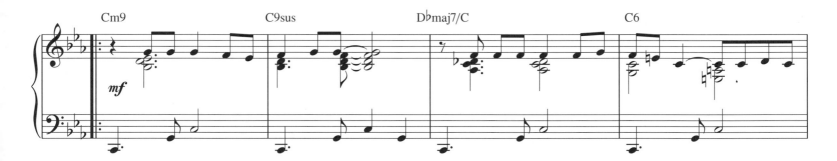

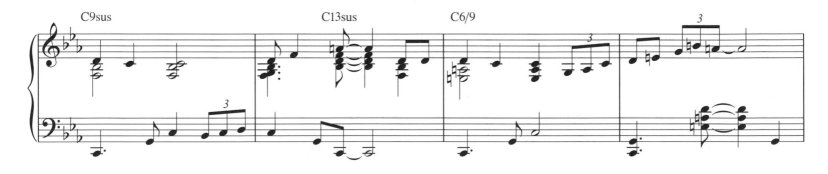

TEACH YOUR CHILDREN

Words and Music by
GRAHAM NASH

Moderately slow bluesy Swing

THAT'S ALL

Words and Music by PHIL COLLINS,
TONY BANKS and MIKE RUTHERFORD

TIN MAN

Words and Music by
DEWEY BUNNELL

VENTURA HIGHWAY

Words and Music by
DEWEY BUNNELL

SISTER GOLDEN HAIR

Words and Music by
GERRY BECKLEY

Freely flowing Jazz Ballad